WEIRDEST
Moments in Sports

by

Marty Gitlin

Printed in the United States of America,
North Mankato, Minnesota
052013
012014

 THIS BOOK CONTAINS AT LEAST 10% RECYCLED MATERIALS.

Editor: Chrös McDougall
Series Designer: Craig Hinton

Photo Credits: Amy Sancetta/AP Images, cover, 1, 5; Jim Mone/AP Images, 7; Fred Jewell/AP Images, 8, 27; AP Images, 11, 24, 30, 36, 58; Denis Poroy/AP Images, 14; Carl Viti/AP Images, 17, 18; Harry Cabluck/AP Images, 21; Bob Jordan/AP Images, 29; John Bazemore/AP Images, 33; Doug Mills/AP Images, 39; Denis Paquin/AP Images, 41; Popperfoto/Getty Images, 42; Koji Sasahara/AP Images, 44; Press Association via AP Images, 46; SIPA/DPPI/Icon SMI, 48; Michael Caulfield/AP Images, 51; Jeff Kowalsky/AP Images, 52; Jack Smith/AP Images, 55; Roberto Pfeil/AP Images, 56

Library of Congress Control Number: 2013932692

Cataloging-in-Publication Data
Gitlin, Marty.
 Weirdest moments in sports / Marty Gitlin.
   p. cm. -- (Sports' biggest moments)
ISBN 978-1-61783-926-9
Includes bibliographical references and index.
1. Sports--Juvenile literature. 2. Sports--Miscellanea--Juvenile literature. I. Title.
796--dc23
                                                                            2013932692

TABLE OF CONTENTS

Chapter 1

WEIRD BASEBALL MOMENTS

They are called midges. Their scientific name is *Chironomus plumosus*. They are tiny insects. And on the muggy evening of October 5, 2007, they were apparently Cleveland Indians fans.

During Game 2 of the American League (AL) Division Series, they were "bugging" the heck out of the visiting New York Yankees.

The swarm descended upon Jacobs Field in Cleveland and attacked Yankees pitcher Joba Chamberlain as he warmed up to start the bottom of the eighth inning. His team was hanging on to a narrow 1–0 lead. Chamberlain had performed brilliantly for New York since being promoted to the majors in early August. There was no reason to believe he would not shut down the Indians. That is, until the midges invaded.

New York Yankees catcher Jorge Posada applies bug spray to pitcher Mariano Rivera during Game 2 of the 2007 AL Division Series.

"I'd never seen anything like it," Yankees shortstop Derek Jeter said. "It's like somebody let them loose. . . . Just when you think you've seen it all."

Trainers sprayed Chamberlain with bug repellent as he took the mound. His teammates began waving their gloves in front of their faces to swat the pests away. It did not work.

The pitcher was clearly irritated. He walked Cleveland hitter Grady Sizemore and threw a wild pitch before being sprayed again. Chamberlain could barely see home plate through the midges. He tossed another wild pitch that allowed Sizemore to score the tying run. The bugs were even getting into his mouth. He was spitting them out. Yet the umpire said he never even thought about stopping the game.

"It was just a little irritation," he said. "We've had bugs before. I've seen bugs and mosquitoes since I've been umpiring. It might not be a perfect scenario."

The midges had done their job for the home team. The Indians won the game. For whatever reason the midges only seemed to greatly affect

Minnesota Twins infielders Houston Jimenez, *right*, and John Castino wait for Dave Kingman's fly ball to drop in 1984.

the game for that short period while the Yankees were pitching. Then Cleveland went on to beat the Yankees in the series. The Indians might not have done so if their tiny friends had not intervened on that fateful night.

Fans storm the field in Chicago as Disco Demolition Night in 1979 turns into a disaster.

Disco Disaster

Chicago White Sox owners Bill Veeck and son Mike Veeck were showmen.

They worked to create strange promotions that would attract fans to

Comiskey Park.

THE INNOVATOR

Bill Veeck was at the end of his career as a baseball owner when he staged the infamous Disco Demolition Night in 1979. He had earned a reputation as one of the most creative thinkers in the sport. His most famous publicity stunt was signing Eddie Gaedel to a contract with the St. Louis Browns in 1951. Veeck shocked everyone in the park by sending the 3-foot-7 Gaedel to bat in a game with the fraction "1/8" as his uniform number. Gaedel walked on four pitches and was removed for a pinch runner. He never appeared in another game.

It appeared on July 12, 1979, that one idea had worked beyond their wildest dreams. It was Disco Demolition Night. The plan was to take advantage of the backlash against disco music, which many fans of rock and roll music hated. The team invited people to bring their disco records to the game. The idea was to blow them up on the field between games of a doubleheader against the Detroit Tigers. Anyone who brought a record got into the game for 98 cents.

The Veecks were thrilled when more than 50,000 fans packed the stadium. But they quickly learned that many fans were not there to simply enjoy a baseball game. As the first game went on the fans became rowdy. Some fans began hurling the records like Frisbees. Some even tossed firecrackers onto the field. Many fans did not care about baseball. They only wanted to create a disturbance.

Finally the first game ended. But after the records were blown up, hordes of young fans ran onto the field. They tore up the bases. They destroyed a batting cage. They set fires. Many of them were arrested. White Sox radio announcer Harry Caray grabbed the field microphone and begged them to return to their seats.

"Holy cow!" he yelled. "Can you hear me out there? To make this an absolutely perfect evening, let's say we all regain our seats, so we can play baseball again!"

His plea was ignored. The umpires declared the field unplayable and forfeited the second game to the Tigers. Mike Veeck had learned a lesson.

"The majority of them didn't come for the ball game," he said. "They came for the happening, and they won't come again. That was my biggest mistake."

Pine Tar Problem

Fiery New York Yankees manager Billy Martin was biding his time. He had suspected for more than a year that Kansas City Royals slugger George Brett was breaking an obscure rule. Martin was just waiting for the perfect time to call Brett on it.

The Kansas City Royals' George Brett, *right*, watches as a policeman leads "The Kissing Bandit" off the field following a kiss in 1977.

That perfect time was the ninth inning of a Yankees-Royals game on July 24, 1983.

Brett had just smashed a two-run homer to give his team a 5–4 lead. Martin turned to Yankees coach Sammy Ellis and winked. Martin walked to home plate umpire Tim McClelland and pointed to Brett's bat lying nearby.

"That bat is illegal," Martin said. "There's too much pine tar. Measure it."

Pine tar is a sticky substance players smear on their bats to get a better grip. However, they are only allowed to put pine tar on certain parts of the bat. McClelland measured Brett's bat and determined that the pine tar was more than 18 inches (45.7 cm) up on the bat. He checked his rule book, strolled to the Royals dugout, and signaled that Brett was out. Since that was the third out of the ninth inning, it meant the Yankees had won the game.

Brett went wild. He sprinted toward McClelland as if he had been shot out of a cannon. He waved his arms and screamed hysterically. The clip of Brett running out of the dugout like a maniac became famous.

But Brett would get the last laugh. AL president Lee MacPhail upheld a Royals protest. He said that the bat should have been removed from the game but the home run should have counted. MacPhail forced the game to be resumed with Kansas City now leading 5–4.

Martin and Yankees owner George Steinbrenner seethed with anger. Steinbrenner took legal steps to stop the game. The New York State Supreme Court issued a court order to prevent it from being completed, but that was overruled.

The game finally continued weeks later. Martin tried to protest by making a joke out of the game. He had first baseman Don Mattingly play second base and pitcher Ron Guidry play center field. Martin then claimed that Brett never touched first base on his trot around the bases on his home run.

His efforts were in vain. Royals closer Dan Quisenberry retired the Yankees on just 10 pitches to complete a game that had started 25 days, 4 hours, and 14 minutes earlier.

The memory of Brett blasting out of his dugout after his home run had been denied? That would last forever.

The Fireballer and the Bird

The dove is a symbol of peace. But what happened to one unlucky dove on March 25, 2001, was not so peaceful.

Arizona Diamondbacks pitcher Randy Johnson fired fastballs as hard as anyone in the sport. They routinely were in the high 90 miles-per-hour (145 km/h) range. Sometimes they even exceeded 100 miles per hour (161 km/h). Johnson hurled one of those pitches in a spring training game that day against the San Francisco Giants. It happened to come at the

Arizona Diamondbacks pitcher Randy Johnson, shown in 2001, was one of the hardest-throwing pitchers in baseball.

exact time that a dove flew between the pitcher's mound and home plate. The pitch slammed straight into the dove.

Feathers blew everywhere.

"I'm sitting there waiting for [the pitch], and I'm expecting to catch the thing, and all you see is an explosion," Diamondbacks catcher Rod Barajas said. "It's crazy."

Giants batter Calvin Murray was equally stunned.

"[The dove] exploded, feathers and everything, just 'poof!'" he said. "There were nothing but feathers lying on home plate. I never saw the ball, nothing but feathers."

One observer joked that the dove should have been wearing a batting helmet. But Johnson was in no mood for humor. He was upset about killing the dove.

"I don't think it was all that funny," he said.

THE FIRST BIRD TO GO

Randy Johnson was not the first baseball player to accidentally kill a bird. During a road game against the Toronto Blue Jays on August 4, 1983, New York Yankees star Dave Winfield tossed a ball to a batboy. It hit a seagull on the head. Winfield was arrested after the game and charged with cruelty to animals. The charges were dropped the next day.

Chapter 2

WEIRD FOOTBALL MOMENTS

The University of Stanford marching band was ready to celebrate. Its team had just taken a 20–19 lead over its archrivals, the University of California. Only four seconds remained in the 1982 game.

Cardinal kicker Mark Harmon squibbed a kickoff. California player Kevin "Moon Dog" Moen fielded it. The Golden Bears realized that if anyone was tackled with the ball, the game would be over and they would be officially beaten. They also knew that it was illegal to pass the ball forward. They had to keep tossing it back to their teammates. And that is just what they did.

The Golden Bears moved the ball up the field. When Moen ran into trouble, he lateraled the ball to Richard Rodgers, who flipped it to Dwight Garner. Three tacklers immediately nailed Garner. It looked like he was

A member of the Stanford band rushes onto the field thinking his team had beaten California in their 1982 game.

The Stanford band celebrates on the field while play is still going on against California in their 1982 game.

down and the game was over. The Stanford band even began to play and march onto the field.

But Garner was not down. He lateraled the ball to Mariet Ford, who tossed it over his head. Moen picked it up and began running. But the Stanford band was in the way. Moen sprinted by the saxophone players. He juked a tuba player. And when he reached the end zone, he flattened trombonist Gary Tyrrell.

Referee Charles Moffett was not even aware that Moen had crossed the goal line. When line judge Gordon Riese informed him, he ruled the touchdown legal. The Golden Bears had won 25–20. Moen was one happy football player.

"Out on the field I was running around hugging all my teammates and they were saying, who scored?" he recalled. "And I said, 'I scored!' Through all that confusion, even I couldn't really tell you what just happened. I knew I had scored, but I didn't know all the pieces that went into play. It was chaotic and so much fun to celebrate with all the students."

The wild finish would forever be known simply as "The Play."

The Immaculate Reception

The Pittsburgh Steelers had been terrible for years. They had managed just seven winning seasons from 1933 to 1971. They were one of the worst teams in the National Football League (NFL).

Their fortunes had finally changed in 1972. They had won 11 of 14 games. That earned the Steelers a first-round playoff game against the talented Oakland Raiders. But Pittsburgh appeared doomed after falling behind 7–6 with just 90 seconds left. The Steelers got the ball back. But soon it was fourth-and-10 from their own 40-yard line with 22 seconds left in the game.

Pittsburgh quarterback Terry Bradshaw dropped back to pass. He scrambled to avoid a fierce Raiders rush. He then heaved the ball down the middle of the field toward running back John "Frenchy" Fuqua.

Fuqua collided with Oakland defensive back Jack Tatum as it arrived. Nobody is sure what happened next. Did the ball bounce off Tatum, Fuqua, or both at the same time? All that can be known for certain is that the ball caromed back to Steelers star halfback Franco Harris. He snagged it from his shoe top and sprinted into the end zone for the game-winning touchdown with five seconds left. It would be dubbed "The Immaculate Reception" because it seemed like a miracle.

Tatum argued that only Fuqua touched the ball. That would have made the catch illegal. NFL rules at the time stated that a receiver could not catch a pass last touched by another offensive player. However,

Franco Harris of the Pittsburgh Steelers runs for a touchdown after making the "Immaculate Reception" in 1972.

replays indicated that Fuqua touched the ball first, but then Tatum indeed made contact with the ball. Because the referees ruled that Tatum touched it last before Harris, the play stood.

"What makes the play great is the mystery of it," said Neil Zender, who later produced a documentary about one of the strangest moments in sports history. "The Raiders see it as a crime, and the Steelers can see it as the hand of God."

Whatever it was, it certainly signaled the beginning of a dynasty. The Steelers did not suffer through another losing season until 1985, and they emerged as the first six-time Super Bowl champion after winning Super Bowl XLIII following the 2008 season.

Woody . . . or Would He Not?

Ohio State University football coach Woody Hayes was known for his temper. He had flown into one rage after another and had even punched a television cameraman in the stomach. It seemed inevitable that his angry outbursts would eventually cost him his job.

The legendary coach met his professional demise on December 29, 1978. Ohio State was trailing the Clemson University Tigers 17–15 in the annual Gator Bowl. His Buckeyes had driven to the Tigers' 24-yard-line. Then Ohio State quarterback Art Schlichter threw an interception to Charlie Bauman.

Hayes lost control when Bauman was tackled near the Ohio State bench. He grabbed the shocked Bauman and hit him with his forearm. Hayes then attacked his own player, Ken Fritz, who had attempted to calm him down. The Buckeyes were penalized 15 yards for Hayes's actions. They were penalized 15 more when he ran onto the field and had to be escorted away by an assistant coach.

Ohio State Athletic Director Hugh Hindman informed Hayes after the game that he "could expect the worst possible result" from the incident and that he was welcome to resign. But Hayes refused.

TOO OLD TO PLAY BY THEN

The Philadelphia Eagles picked Syracuse fullback Norm Michael in the eighteenth round of the 1944 NFL Draft. There was just one problem: Michael never found out until 1999. He discovered it that year by reading a list in the newspaper of every Syracuse player ever drafted.

"My son sent [the Eagles] a letter after we found out," Michael said. "I think he wanted to see if the Eagles owed me a signing bonus. Think of the interest I could have [accumulated on the money]. Fifty-seven years worth."

Ohio State coach Woody Hayes grabs his own player after punching a Clemson player in the 1978 Gator Bowl.

"I'm not going to resign," Hayes replied. "That would make it too easy for you. You had better go ahead and fire me."

That is what happened. It did not matter that he had been coaching the Buckeyes since 1951. It did not matter that he had led the Buckeyes to the Rose Bowl eight times and to five national titles.

"There isn't a university or athletic conference in the country which would permit a coach to physically assault a college athlete," said Ohio State president Harold L. Enarson just before he fired Hayes.

Johnson to Johnson

Every touchdown pass in the history of the NFL has been thrown and caught by two different players. Well, all but one.

The exception took place on October 12, 1997. That was when Minnesota Vikings quarterback Brad Johnson tossed a pass intended for tight end Andrew Glover. Carolina Panthers nose tackle Greg Kragen batted it down.

There was nothing too unusual about that. But what happened next was downright wild. The ball landed right back in the hands of Johnson. He weaved past defenders into the end zone for the score. He had thrown a touchdown pass to himself.

"Oh, that's been in the playbook forever," Vikings offensive tackle Todd Steussie joked. "We just haven't called it."

The Elias Sports Bureau scrambled to find another play in NFL history in which the touchdown passer and receiver was the same person. It found no other examples. And better yet for Johnson, his heroics had given his team the lead in a 21–14 victory.

Minnesota Vikings quarterback Brad Johnson prepares to pass the ball against the Chicago Bears in a 1997 game.

Chapter 3

WEIRD BASKETBALL MOMENTS

Indiana University basketball coach Bobby Knight was angry. There was nothing unusual about that. He had the most notorious temper in the sport. But on February 23, 1985, he was even more upset than usual. His Hoosiers had fallen behind 11–2 to in-state rival Purdue University. The Boilermakers were embarrassing Knight's Hoosiers on their home court.

One could sense that Knight was about to explode. He leaped off the bench to argue when a foul was called on Indiana guard Steve Alford. Less than a minute later, the official whistled a foul on Hoosiers player Marty Simmons. Knight protested again, screaming at the referee. Seconds later yet another call went against his team, this time on Daryl Thomas.

Knight became furious. He swore and screamed at official Fred Jaspers, who called a technical foul on him. That was all Knight could take. He picked up a red plastic chair from the Hoosiers' bench and heaved it

28

Indiana coach Bobby Knight was known for his fiery temper during his 29 seasons coaching the Hoosiers.

across the court. The chair twisted and slid toward the wheelchair section of the arena. The chair came to a rest just a few feet away from fans sitting in wheelchairs. Everyone on the court was stunned. Jaspers slapped Knight with another technical foul and ejected him from the game.

Indiana players had grown accustomed to watching Knight lose his temper in practices, but not in front of thousands of fans. Knight said he instinctively wanted to show his anger by tearing off his suit jacket. "But I wasn't wearing a jacket, so I grabbed a chair instead," he explained.

Knight apologized the next day, but it was too late. His reputation as a hothead had gained strength.

Wrong-Way Warren

The 1970–71 Cleveland Cavaliers were the joke of the National Basketball Association (NBA). They had tied a league record by losing their first 15 games. That they were an expansion team was no excuse. The Buffalo Braves and Portland Trail Blazers were also in their first seasons, and they were performing far better.

Fans were laughing at the Cavaliers. But they never laughed as hard as they did on December 9, 1970. A meager crowd of 2,022 was in attendance at the creaky old Cleveland Arena as the Cavaliers played the Trail Blazers. The Cavaliers were losing as usual, but they were at least competitive on this night. They trailed just 84–81 after three quarters.

Cleveland guard Bobby Lewis secured the tip to start the fourth quarter. He noticed fellow guard John Warren running toward the basket

THE NOT-SO-GREAT SHOE TOSS

Bill Walton was among the greatest centers in NBA history. He was also a free spirit. He proved it when his shoe came off in a game during the 1984-85 season while he was playing for the Los Angeles Clippers. Rather than try to put it back on, he tossed it into the air at a shot taken by Los Angeles Lakers forward Bob McAdoo. The silliness drew the attention of referee Earl Strom, who called a technical foul on Walton. According to Walton, Strom called the foul for "violating the spirit of the rules of the game."

and threw him a perfect pass. Warren laid the ball in. There was only one problem.

It was the *wrong basket*. Warren had put the ball into the Portland hoop. The official blew his whistle and ordered that two points be given to the Trail Blazers.

"I thought I had a basket," Warren told the *Cleveland Plain Dealer*. "When I heard the whistle, I thought I had been called for traveling or something."

Lewis played his part in the debacle.

"When I see a gold shirt going to the basket, I throw it to him," he said.

And when Portland center LeRoy Ellis saw a gold shirt going to the basket, he reacted as well. Ignorant to the fact that Warren was about to score two points for the Trail Blazers, he tried to block the shot. Instead,

NOW THAT'S THE SPIRIT!

Spirit is the name of a bird that flies down from the rafters during player introductions before Atlanta Hawks home games. But the bird wanted to hog more attention before a playoff game on April 23, 2009.

The Zoo Atlanta resident perched himself atop the scoreboard and refused to leave. The hawk then flew around the arena during the first quarter before landing on top of the Atlanta basket. The game was halted for more than eight minutes as his handler arrived and carried him out of the arena to the cheers of fans and players.

The Atlanta Hawks' mascot, Spirit, perches on the shot clock during the team's 2009 playoff game against the Miami Heat.

he received credit for the two points because he was the Portland player closest to the play.

The oddities of that game were not over. The Blazers were later called for a technical foul for having six players on the court.

The Fouling Machine

Nobody was about to mistake Bubba Wells for Michael Jordan or any other NBA superstar. He was a rookie playing around 10 minutes per game for the lowly Dallas Mavericks in 1997–98. The Mavericks had lost every game but one in which Wells had played.

It was December 29, 1997. The Mavericks were playing the eventual NBA champion Chicago Bulls. Dallas coach Don Nelson told Wells to enter late in the game and carry out a special task. He wanted Wells to keep fouling forward Dennis Rodman. Rodman was a famously terrible free throw shooter.

It seemed like a good plan. Nelson figured that Rodman would miss most of his shots. Meanwhile sacrificing Wells would allow the more

WHAT? TOILET PAPER?

John Brown University is a tiny school in Siloam Springs, Arkansas. But it is noteworthy for one strange basketball tradition. After the team scores its first points every season, the fans celebrate by throwing rolls of toilet paper onto the court. The Golden Eagles mascot then dances as the paper-tossing fans cheer before the mess is cleaned up.

important Mavericks players to keep their foul totals down. Wells was expendable. He was so expendable that Nelson did not mind that he set an NBA record by committing six fouls and fouling out in 3:00.

"He came up to me and asked me if I wanted to do it," Wells said of Nelson several years later. "I said if it helps the team win, I'll do it. I had no clue about setting a record or anything like that."

He also had no clue that Rodman would ruin the strategy by making 9 of 12 of his free throws after the Wells fouls to clinch a 111–105 victory for the Bulls.

"It's not a record I'm happy with," Wells said after the game. "I guess I took one for the team."

The team needed all the help it could get. The Mavericks finished the season with a terrible 20–62 record.

Gold Heist in Germany

The strangest ending in Olympic basketball history occurred in the championship game between the United States and the Soviet Union on September 10, 1972, in Munich, West Germany. And it cost the Americans a gold medal.

Team USA had overcome a 10-point deficit to take a 50–49 lead on two foul shots by Doug Collins. Soviet coach Vladimir Kondrashin then raced onto the court to call timeout. The rules stated he should have been called for a technical foul for leaving the bench area, but he was not. It did

US basketball players celebrate after they thought they had won the Olympic gold medal in 1972.

not seem to matter when the Soviets missed a last-second shot. The US players celebrated what they believed had been a gold-medal victory.

The referees had other ideas. The Soviet Union's coach claimed he had called a timeout with three seconds left to play. The referees upheld that claim and told the Americans that they were giving the Soviets three seconds to try again. They warned the US players that they would forfeit the game if they did not return to the court.

Hurried US coach Hank Iba left 7-foot-2 Tom Burleson on the bench rather than putting him in the game to guard against a long pass. Then 6-foot-8 Soviet star Alexander Belov out-jumped two shorter American defenders under the basket and scored the winning basket. Now it was the Soviets celebrating a gold medal triumph.

The US players were heartbroken and angry. They have refused to this day to accept their silver medals.

Chapter 4

WEIRD OLYMPIC MOMENTS

Nancy Kerrigan could never have imagined that violence and tragedy awaited her on the snowy Thursday afternoon of January 6, 1994. She had just completed a practice session the day before the start of the US Figure Skating Championships in Detroit. Security at Cobo Arena was laid-back. Anyone could walk through the hallways without showing credentials.

And on this day, anyone did. Kerrigan had stopped for an interview. A man pointed to her and asked figure skating coach Frank Carroll if that was indeed Kerrigan. Carroll considered it weird, but he nodded his head.

"I thought, 'This is strange,'" Carroll said. "He was an odd man. He was jittery, sweating. He had a camera and was taking pictures, very fast. . . . The next thing I knew, Nancy was on the floor screaming."

US figure skaters Nancy Kerrigan, *left*, and Tonya Harding, *right*, captivated the world at the 1994 Olympic Winter Games.

The man wearing a black leather jacket, black hat, and khaki pants had run toward Kerrigan and smashed her right knee with a metal pipe. Kerrigan collapsed, screamed three times, and began crying uncontrollably.

"It hurts so bad," she shrieked. "Please help me. . . . I'm so scared. Why me? Why now? Why?"

Why Nancy Kerrigan? An investigation proved the attack was set up by a thug named Jeff Gillooly. He was the ex-husband of Tonya Harding, who was a chief figure skating rival of Kerrigan. Gillooly and three friends had planned the attack and carried it out to ensure that Kerrigan could not compete in the championships or the Olympic Winter Games that year.

Harding was never proven to have known about the attack. However, she admitted that she failed to report what she knew about the perpetrators after the deed was done.

With Kerrigan sidelined, Harding won the US Championships. Kerrigan recovered in time to skate at the Olympics in Lillehammer, Norway. She had become beloved and admired while Harding had emerged as a villain. Americans rooted hard for Kerrigan and against Harding in the Olympics. The broadcasts of the 1994 Olympic figure skating competition remain some of the most-watched shows of all time—it even had better TV ratings than most Super Bowls through 2013.

Kerrigan fans were rewarded. She performed splendidly and won a silver medal. Harding skated terribly and finished eighth.

US figure skater Nancy Kerrigan, *right*, poses with the other medalists at the 1994 Olympic Winter Games in Lillehammer, Norway.

One month later Harding was convicted of conspiracy to hinder the prosecution of Gillooly and the others. She was banned for life from US figure skating events. She later resurfaced in the early 2000s as a boxer.

Duck, Duck, No Goose

Australian Robert Henry Pearce was either a duck lover or he felt certain of winning his quarterfinal race in the sculling event at the 1928 Olympic Games in Amsterdam, Netherlands. Or both.

Robert Henry Pearce receives a laurel after winning a rowing gold medal in the 1928 Olympic Games in Amsterdam, Netherlands.

Pearce was receiving heavy competition from French rower Victor Saurin, but that did not stop him from halting when a family of ducks passed in front of him single file. Pearce then sculled to victory, much to the delight of the Dutch onlookers and animal lovers.

The ducks remained unharmed—and so did Pearce in his quest for a gold medal. He won the event easily. Pearce defeated US rower Kenneth Myers in the finals by a stunning margin of 9.8 seconds.

Pearce struggled to find work in Australia during the Great Depression of the early 1930s. However, he recovered to represent his country again in the 1932 Olympic Games held in Los Angeles. There he held off American William Miller to become the first rower to win a second singles sculling gold medal.

There were no reports of Pearce stopping to allow ducks to swim by in that event.

Hey, Tackling Belongs in Football

Brazilian Vanderlei de Lima had a goal. He wanted to become the first runner from his country to win the Olympic marathon event. And he

Defrocked Irish priest Cornelius Horan grabs Brazilian marathon runner Vanderlei de Lima during the 2004 Olympic marathon.

was in sight of that goal with less than 4 miles (6.4 km) to go in the 2004 Olympic Games held in Athens, Greece.

De Lima was leading the pack when he saw a shocking sight in front of him. It was a drunken stranger named Cornelius Horan, a former Irish priest who had been forced to leave the priesthood. Horan pushed de Lima off the road. De Lima recovered, but he was passed by two other runners and forced to take the third-place bronze medal.

"If that spectator didn't jump in front of me in the middle of the race, who knows what would have happened?" asked a frustrated de Lima. "Maybe I would have won. It disturbed me a lot."

Horan was arrested and taken to the police station. He provided a strange explanation to police for his actions. Horan stated that he pushed de Lima to prepare for the second coming of Jesus Christ. The police also learned that Horan had interrupted the British Formula One Grand Prix auto race in 2003 by jumping onto the track.

MIND YOUR OWN BEESWAX!

Portuguese marathon runner Francisco Lazaro wanted to win his event in the 1912 Olympic Games in Stockholm, Sweden. He also wanted to avoid sunburn. So he smeared beeswax on his body to keep the sun from burning his skin. Bad move. Lazaro dropped dead en route to the finish line. The original cause of death was ruled as severe dehydration. It was later discovered that the tragedy was the result of the beeswax. It had clogged his pores and prevented him from sweating.

Italy's Dorando Pietri is illegally helped across the marathon finish line at the 1904 Olympic Games in London, England.

The International Olympic Committee (IOC) presented de Lima with a sportsmanship award for "exceptional demonstration of fair play and Olympic values." The award is called the Pierre de Coubertin Medal, named after the founder of the modern Olympic Games.

The Faulty Vault

Timing is critical in gymnastics. So when the vault was curiously set 2 inches (5 cm) too low in the first two rounds of the all-around competition at the 2000 Olympic Games in Sydney, Australia, the result was disastrous.

One by one, the female gymnasts attempted to launch themselves up with their hands only to miss the vault completely or hit it too lightly and fall awkwardly to the floor. Many limped away in pain, frustration, and anger. It was not until gymnast Allana Slater of Australia asked for a measurement that the vault height was measured. It was then discovered to be two inches shorter than the required 49 (125 cm) inches tall.

By then it was too late. The vault was raised, but the timing had been lost for many of the participants. Perhaps the most frustrated was former world champion Svetlana Khorkina. She had crashed to the floor and bumped her head during the faulty vault competition. She was never the

Andreea Raducan of Romania was one of few
gymnasts who had success on vault at the
2000 Olympic Games. She won all-around gold.

same. The flustered Russian proceeded to fall on the uneven bars. That was usually her best event.

US television analyst and former Olympic gold medalist Peter Vidmar understood what happened to Khorkina. "It's like she said, 'Welcome to my nightmare,'" Vidmar explained. "When she blew the vault, the tears came. She knew it was all over. When she got on the uneven bars, all the wind was out of her sails."

Olympic officials allowed the victims of the short vault to take their turns over. But by that time Khorkina was out of the running for a medal and declined to try again. The Romanian gymnasts handled the situation far better. They won the all-around gold, silver, and bronze medals. That made Romania the first country to sweep since the Soviet Union did so in 1960.

Chapter 5

OTHER WEIRD MOMENTS

The achievement of scoring three goals in a National Hockey League (NHL) game has been known as a "hat trick" since the 1940s. But after one fateful home game for the Florida Panthers in 1995, a two-goal game became known as a "rat trick." And it would lead to one of the strangest episodes in league history.

It all began innocently enough when the Panthers awaited their home opener in their locker room. They were startled when a rat scurried across the floor. Right wing Scott Mellanby killed the rat by slamming it against the wall with his stick. Mellanby later scored two goals that night to lead the Panthers to victory. Afterward, teammate John Vanbiesbrouck exclaimed jokingly that Mellanby had registered a "rat trick."

The phrase caught on. Fans purchased rubber and plastic rats by the thousands. They tossed them on the ice to celebrate Panthers goals.

Scott Mellanby of the Florida Panthers, *left,* became known for inciting the "rat trick."

While throwing rats onto NHL rinks is uncommon, Detroit Red Wings fans sometimes throw octopi onto the rink for good luck.

They sneaked the rats past security and into the arena. It took an army of 40 arena attendants sponsored by the Orkin exterminator company to clean up the fake rats that littered the playing surface. Supermarkets in Miami were selling "rat cakes" with frosting drawings of rats on them. The rat was all the rage.

The rat craze grew as the surprising Panthers roared into the playoffs. After one Panthers goal in a playoff game against the Pittsburgh Penguins, an estimated 3,000 rats were launched from the stands onto the ice—some of them with fake fur!

"There are the rubber ones, the plastic ones, and these kind of furry ones that some people throw," attendant Jodi Reiter said. "The furry ones are the ones you don't really want to touch. . . . They're too real. Creepy."

The topper? The year 1996, in which the "rat-infested" Panthers steamrolled into the Stanley Cup Finals, was the "Year of the Rat" according to Chinese astrology.

AN UNPLANNED GREAT GOLF SHOT

Golfing great Gene Sarazen did not always hit wonderful shots. But in the 1931 Ryder Cup, even his terrible drive turned out just fine. Sarazen slammed his tee shot well off course. It landed in a refreshment stand. It bounced into a groove on the concrete floor, through an open window, and onto the green. The ball landed just 8 feet from the cup. It was that kind of luck, as well as his talent, that allowed Sarazen to win his match over Fred Robson.

Chomp!

Heavyweight boxing champion Evander Holyfield pointed at the mouth of opponent Mike Tyson and glared at referee Mills Lane. Holyfield wondered why Tyson was not wearing his mouthpiece coming out for the third round of their fight on June 28, 1997, in Las Vegas.

Lane ordered Tyson back to his corner to put in his mouthpiece. Soon everyone would know why Tyson was not wearing it in the first place.

Tyson had once been on top of the boxing world but was beginning to decline. Holyfield was dominating the fight through the first two rounds. Tyson was growing increasingly angry and frustrated with the beating from Holyfield. So with 40 seconds remaining in the third round, he spit out his mouthpiece and got Holyfield in a clinch. Tyson then performed perhaps the most shocking act in sports history. He bit off a chunk of Holyfield's right ear and spit it out in the ring. A stunned Holyfield pushed Tyson away and jumped up and down in pain.

WHAT A KNOCKOUT!

Heavyweight Henry Wallitsch was a mediocre boxer. He managed a career record of 14–13. But he certainly made a name for himself during a fight with Bartolo Soni on September 12, 1959. That was the day that Wallitsch knocked himself out. In the third round, Wallitsch threw a punch at Soni and missed badly. The force of the punch sent Wallitsch over the ropes and onto the concrete floor. He was knocked cold. It was the only time a fighter has ever been responsible for his own knockout.

Mike Tyson bites into the ear of Evander Holyfield during their heavyweight boxing match in 1997 in Las Vegas.

Lane stopped the fight as blood poured from what was left of Holyfield's ear. Holyfield turned his back on Tyson, who attacked him from behind and pushed him into the ropes. Lane finally stepped in as the blood ran down Holyfield's shoulder and back.

Paul, an octopus at a German aquarium, correctly picks that Spain would beat the Netherlands in the 2010 World Cup final.

The referee considered stopping the fight. Instead he merely deducted two points from Tyson's score and allowed it to resume. Soon Tyson was biting off a chunk of Holyfield's *left* ear. Tyson had flown into a rage. He tried to punch a police officer who had entered the ring as

PAUL THE PROPHET

What would a typical octopus know about soccer? Usually, nothing. But an England-born octopus named Paul had an incredible knack for predicting the results of soccer matches. Paul lived at the Sea Life aquarium in Oberhausen, Germany. He correctly picked the winner of all seven matches involving the German team in the 2010 World Cup by choosing to eat a mussel from boxes showing the German flag or that of its opponent. The team on the box that Paul ate from won on each occasion. Paul became more and more famous with each correct pick. He then successfully picked the Spain victory over the Netherlands in the final.

bedlam broke loose. Public address announcer Jimmy Lennon Jr. then read a decision that one could never imagine hearing.

"Referee Mills Lane has disqualified Mike Tyson for biting Evander Holyfield on both of his ears," Lennon said.

Fans pelted Tyson with cups of beer and soda. Police arrested unruly fans. Tyson returned their anger with an obscene gesture. He attempted to climb into the stands for more brawling before being restrained and dragged into his locker room.

Holyfield was treated by a plastic surgeon at the hospital to repair his ear. He was still heavyweight champion, but keeping his crown came at quite a cost.

Pickles the Hero Mutt

It all started on March 20, 1966. The soccer World Cup's Jules Rimet Trophy was stolen from a hall in Westminster, England. The following evening a

England's soccer team celebrates with the famous Jules Rimet Trophy after winning the 1966 World Cup.

South London resident named David Corbett left his apartment to make a phone call from a kiosk down the road. With him was his four-year-old dog Pickles.

Pickles was not originally Corbett's dog. Corbett had taken the mutt as a puppy from his brother, who complained that Pickles had been chewing on his furniture. Corbett was certainly happy he had taken control of Pickles on that fateful evening. The dog drew his attention to a package wrapped in a newspaper. The package was lying in front of the front wheel of his neighbor's car. Corbett tore it open to reveal a stunning surprise.

He rushed inside his home. "I've found the World Cup! I've found the World Cup!" he shouted to his wife.

Pickles was treated like a hero. He starred in a feature film titled *The Spy with the Cold Nose* and appeared on several television programs. He was named Dog of the Year in Britain and given a free supply of food. Offers poured in from Chile, Czechoslovakia, and Germany to visit those countries. When England won the World Cup that year, Pickles earned an invitation to a celebration banquet.

Alas, his life was cut short. A year later, he got away from Corbett's six-year-old son to chase a cat. His chain was tangled around a tree and he choked to death. Pickles was gone, but his heroics lived on in the hearts and minds of soccer fans throughout the world.

FUN FACTS

★ During a May 1993 Major League Baseball game at Cleveland Stadium, a ball hit by Indians player Carlos Martinez bounced off the head of Texas Rangers outfielder Jose Canseco and over the fence for a home run.

★ The first modern Olympic Games was held in 1896 in Athens, Greece. Australian marathon runner Edwin Flack had his butler pedal a bicycle beside him to provide him with refreshments. The plan failed because the butler—not Flack—collapsed.

★ Miami Dolphins kicker Garo Yepremian tossed the worst pass ever thrown in the Super Bowl. He picked up the ball after his field goal attempt was blocked. Instead of falling on it to preserve a 14–0 lead, he tried to throw it. The pass was intercepted and returned for a touchdown. However, Miami still won.

★ During the 1956 Olympic Games in Australia, Russian rower Vyacheslav Ivanov celebrated after winning his first Olympic gold medal by leaping. The medal fell into Lake Wendouree, never to be found.

★ Detroit Red Wings hockey fans began a tradition in 1952 of throwing octopi on the ice for good luck. The octopus' eight legs represented the number of playoff wins a team needed to win the Stanley Cup at the time. During one 1995 game, fans tossed 36 octopi on the playing surface.

★ Romanian tennis star Ilie Nastase, known for his clownish behavior on the court, once held up an umbrella while playing at the 1974 Wimbledon Championships. He was angry that the match had not been halted in the rain.

GLOSSARY

ARCHRIVALS
The one opposing team that brings out the most passion from a team and its fans.

DRAFT
A system used by professional sports teams to spread incoming talent throughout the league.

EXPANSION TEAM
A team playing its first year in a league.

GROUND-RULE DOUBLE
A hit in baseball in which the batter is awarded second base after his hit has become unplayable, such as when it bounces over the fence.

LATERAL
A short pass that goes behind the ball carrier in football.

MASCOT
A person, animal, or character that represents a sports team.

PLAYOFFS
A series of games played to determine a champion in a particular sport.

PROMOTION
A special event used at a sporting event to attract more fans.

SCULLING
A type of rowing sport.

SQUIB
A short, low kick used in football when the kicking team wants to avoid kicking to the primary return man.

TECHNICAL FOUL
A foul called by a referee in basketball for a grievous verbal or physical act.

WILD PITCH
A pitch that generally cannot be handled by a catcher and allows a runner to advance.

FOR MORE INFORMATION

Selected Bibliography

Associated Press. "Bugs help Tribe rally to win in 11, take 2-0 lead." *ESPN*. ESPN Internet Ventures. 5 Oct. 2007. Web. 12 April 2013.

Fischer, David. "Take My Record, Please." *The New York Times*. The New York Times Company. 15 May 2005. Web. 12 April 2013.

Mihoces, Gary. "Immaculate Reception turns 40; debate lives." *USA Today*. Gannett. 18 Dec. 2012. Web. 12 April 2013.

Montville, Leigh. "Rat Pack." *SI Vault*. Time Inc. 10 June 1996. Web. 12 April 2013.

Further Readings

Christopher, Matt. *Great Moments in the Summer Olympics*. New York: Little, Brown Books for Young Readers, 2012.

Corr Morse, Jenifer. *Scholastic Book of World Records, 2013*. New York: Scholastic Paperbacks, 2012.

Martirano, Ron. *Book of Baseball Stuff: Great Records, Weird Happenings, Odd Facts, Amazing Moments & Cool Things*. Watertown, MA: Imprint! Publishing, 2009.

Teitelbaum, Michael. *Weird Sports*. Santa Barbara, CA: Beach Ball Books, 2011.

Web Links

To learn more about the weirdest moments in sports, visit ABDO Publishing Company online at **www.abdopublishing.com**. Web sites about the weirdest moments in sports are featured on our Book Links page. These links are routinely monitored and updated to provide the most current information available.

Places to Visit

Naismith Memorial Basketball Hall of Fame
1000 Hall Fame Ave
Springfield, MA 01105
(413) 781-6500
www.hoophall.com
The Naismith Memorial Basketball Hall of Fame honors basketball's greatest players and moments.

National Baseball Hall of Fame and Museum
25 Main Street
Cooperstown, NY 13326
(888) 425-5633
www.baseballhall.org
This hall of fame and museum highlights the greatest players and moments in the history of baseball.

Pro Football Hall of Fame
2121 George Halas Drive NW
Canton, OH 44708
(330) 456-8207
www.profootballhof.com
This hall of fame and museum highlights the greatest players and moments in the history of the NFL.

INDEX

About the Author

Marty Gitlin is a freelance writer based in Cleveland, Ohio. He has written more than 70 educational books, including a wide variety about the world of sports. Gitlin has won more than 45 awards during his 30 years as a writer, including first place for general excellence from the Associated Press. He lives with his wife and three children.